AUSTRIA 2016 HUMAN RIGHTS REPORT

EXECUTIVE SUMMARY

The Republic of Austria is a parliamentary democracy with constitutional power shared between a popularly elected president and a bicameral parliament (federal assembly). The multiparty parliament and the coalition government it elects exercise most day-to-day governmental powers. National parliamentary elections in 2013 and presidential elections in 2016 were considered free and fair. In July the Constitutional Court found procedural irregularities in the second-round runoff vote of the presidential election held in May but no evidence of manipulation of ballots; in December there was a repeat of the runoff vote.

Civilian authorities maintained effective control over the security forces.

The most significant human rights problem in the country remained societal discrimination against ethnic minorities, including Muslims, immigrants, Roma, Jews, and foreigners of African origin.

The law limits freedom of speech by forbidding both denial of Nazi genocide and hate speech based on race, nationality, religion, or ethnicity. There were some anti-Semitic incidents, including physical attacks, taunting, property damage, and vilifying or threatening letters and telephone calls. Laws mandating access for persons with disabilities were not fully enforced.

The government investigated public officials for suspected wrongdoing and punished those who committed abuses.

Section 1. Respect for the Integrity of the Person, Including Freedom from:

a. Arbitrary Deprivation of Life and other Unlawful or Politically Motivated Killings

There were no reports that the government or its agents committed arbitrary or unlawful killings.

b. Disappearance

There were no reports of politically motivated disappearances.

c. Torture and Other Cruel, Inhuman, or Degrading Treatment or Punishment

The law prohibits such practices, but there were some reports that police used excessive force with detainees and psychiatric patients.

In November 2015 the Council of Europe's Committee for the Prevention of Torture (CPT) released a report on its 2014 visit to police establishments, prisons, and a psychiatric establishment in the country. While the vast majority of detainees interviewed by the CPT had been treated correctly by police, the CPT also received a few allegations of excessive use of force.

The government investigated allegations of such practices and prosecuted cases in which credible evidence existed. In March a Vienna court acquitted a police officer charged with bodily injury when he apprehended a suspected pickpocket in July 2015. The officer asserted that he had attempted to prevent an attack on his colleague. The Human Rights Advisory Council and the federal ombudsmen monitored police respect for human rights and made recommendations to the minister of the interior.

Prison and Detention Center Conditions

There were no significant reports regarding prison or detention center conditions that raised human rights concerns.

<u>Physical Conditions</u>: The reported incidence of death in prisons and pretrial detention centers was low, although specific numbers were not available. In its November 2015 report, the CPT expressed "serious concern" about the almost total lack of medical confidentiality in all the establishments visited and the fact that prison officers with only basic health care training performed health-related tasks normally reserved for qualified nurses.

In the course of a restructuring of the prison system administration in 2015, a unit in the justice ministry took over the overall management and supervision.

<u>Administration</u>: The government investigated and monitored prison and detention center conditions. The federal ombudsman's office may investigate allegations of inhuman conditions on behalf of prisoners and detainees.

<u>Independent Monitoring</u>: Nongovernmental organizations (NGOs) monitored detainees on a regular basis. Human rights groups continued to criticize the incarceration of nonviolent offenders, including persons awaiting deportation, in single cells or inadequate facilities designed for temporary detention. The CPT conducted periodic visits to the country, most recently in September-October 2014, to examine the treatment of persons in police custody and prison as well as detention center conditions for migrants. The CPT also visited a psychiatric hospital to examine the use of physical restraints.

d. Arbitrary Arrest or Detention

The law prohibits arbitrary arrest and detention, and the government generally observed these prohibitions.

Role of the Police and Security Apparatus

Civilian authorities maintained effective control over the police and army, and the government had effective mechanisms to investigate and punish abuse and corruption. The federal police maintain internal security and report to the Ministry of the Interior. The army is responsible for external security but also has some domestic security responsibilities and reports to the Defense Ministry. The criminal courts are responsible for investigating police violations of the law.

NGOs continued to criticize the police for allegedly targeting minorities for frequent identity checks. Racial sensitivity training for police and other officials continued with NGO assistance.

Arrest Procedures and Treatment of Detainees

Authorities base arrests on sufficient evidence and legal warrants issued by a duly authorized official. Authorities bring the arrested person before an independent judiciary. In criminal cases the law allows investigative or pretrial detention for no more than 48 hours, during which time a judge may decide to grant a prosecution request for extended detention. The law specifies the grounds for investigative detention and conditions for bail. There were strict checks on the enforcement of pretrial detention restrictions and bail provisions, and a judge is required to evaluate investigative detention cases periodically. The maximum duration for investigative detention is two years. There is a functioning bail system. Police and judicial authorities generally respected these laws and procedures. There were isolated reports of police abuse, which authorities investigated and, where warranted, prosecuted.

Detainees have the right to a lawyer. Although indigent criminal suspects have the right to an attorney at government expense, the law requires appointment of an attorney only after a court decision to remand such suspects into custody (96 hours after apprehension). Criminal suspects are not legally required to answer questions without an attorney present. Laws providing for compensation for persons unlawfully detained were enforced.

In its November 2015 report, the CPT found it unacceptable that authorities were continuing the practice of subjecting juveniles, some as young as 14, to police questioning and asking them to sign statements without a lawyer or a trusted person present. The report also noted that indigent persons could not usually benefit from the presence of a lawyer during police questioning.

<u>Detainee's Ability to Challenge Lawfulness of Detention before a Court</u>: Persons arrested on criminal charges are entitled to challenge the arrest in court and can obtain prompt release and compensation if found to have been unlawfully detained.

<u>Protracted Detention of Rejected Asylum Seekers or Stateless Persons</u>: In rare cases authorities detained unsuccessful applicants for asylum pending deportation. Some NGOs criticized the government for protracted detention in such cases. The government provided free legal counsel for persons awaiting deportation.

e. Denial of Fair Public Trial

The law provides for an independent judiciary, and the government generally respected judicial independence.

Trial Procedures

The law provides for the right to a fair public trial, and an independent judiciary generally enforced this right.

The law presumes persons charged with criminal offenses are innocent until proven guilty; authorities inform them promptly and in detail of the charges. Trials must be public and conducted orally; defendants have the right to be present at their trial. Attorneys are not mandatory in cases of minor offenses, but legal counsel is available at no charge for needy persons in cases where attorneys are mandatory. The law grants defendants and their attorneys adequate time and facilities to prepare a defense and access to government-held evidence relevant to their cases. Defendants can confront or question witnesses against them and present witnesses and evidence on their own behalf. Free interpretation is available from the moment a defendant is charged, through all appeals. Suspects cannot be compelled to testify or confess guilt. A system of judicial review provides multiple opportunities for appeal.

The law extends the above rights to all defendants regardless of sex, gender, race, ethnicity, age, religion, or mental or physical disability.

Political Prisoners and Detainees

There were no reports of political prisoners or detainees.

Civil Judicial Procedures and Remedies

There is an independent and impartial judiciary in civil matters, including an appellate system. These institutions are accessible to plaintiffs seeking damages for human rights violations. Administrative and judicial remedies were available for redressing alleged wrongs. Individuals and organizations may appeal domestic decisions to regional human rights bodies.

f. Arbitrary or Unlawful Interference with Privacy, Family, Home, or Correspondence

The law prohibits such actions, and there were no reports the government failed to respect these prohibitions.

Section 2. Respect for Civil Liberties, Including:

a. Freedom of Speech and Press

The constitution provides for freedom of speech and press, and the government generally respected these rights. An independent press, an effective judiciary, and a functioning democratic political system combined to promote freedom of speech and the press.

Freedom of Speech and Expression: The law prohibits incitement, insult, or contempt against a group because of its members' race, nationality, religion, or ethnicity if the statement violates human dignity, and imposes criminal penalties for violations. The government strictly enforced these laws (see section 6, Anti-Semitism).

<u>Press and Media Freedoms</u>: The law prohibits public denial, belittlement, approval, or justification of the Nazi genocide or other Nazi crimes against humanity in print media, broadcast media, the publication of books, and online newspapers or journals, and provides criminal penalties for violations. The government strictly enforced these laws (see section 6, Anti-Semitism).

<u>Libel/Slander Laws</u>: Strict libel and slander laws created conditions that discouraged reporting of governmental abuse. For example, many observers believed the ability and willingness of police to sue for libel or slander discouraged individuals from reporting police abuses.

Internet Freedom

With limited exceptions, the government did not restrict or disrupt access to the internet or censor online content, and there were no credible reports the government monitored private online communications without appropriate legal authority. Authorities continued to restrict access to websites containing information that violated the law, such as neo-Nazi sites. The law barring neo-Nazi activity provides for one- to 10-year prison sentences for public denial, belittlement, approval, or justification of National Socialist crimes. The criminal code provision on incitement provides for prison sentences of up to five years. Authorities restricted access to prohibited websites by trying to shut them down and by forbidding the country's internet service providers from carrying them.

Academic Freedom and Cultural Events

There were no government restrictions on academic freedom or cultural events.

b. Freedom of Peaceful Assembly and Association

The law provides for the freedoms of assembly and association, and the government generally respected these rights.

c. Freedom of Religion

See the Department of State's *International Religious Freedom Report* at
www.state.gov/religiousfreedomreport/.

**d. Freedom of Movement, Internally Displaced Persons, Protection of
Refugees, and Stateless Persons**

The law provides for freedom of internal movement, foreign travel, emigration,
and repatriation, and the government generally respected these rights.

The government cooperated with the Office of the UN High Commissioner for
Refugees (UNHCR) and other humanitarian organizations in providing protection
and assistance to refugees, asylum seekers, stateless persons, or other persons of
concern.

In-country Movement: Asylum seekers' freedom of movement was restricted to
the district of the reception center where authorities assigned them for the duration
of their initial application process until the country's responsibility for examining
the application was determined. By law asylum seekers must be physically present
in the centers of first reception for up to 120 hours during the initial application
process. Authorities have 20 days in which to determine the country's
responsibility and jurisdiction and whether they have purview.

Protection of Refugees

Access to Asylum: The law provides for the granting of asylum or refugee status,
and the government established a system for providing protection to refugees.

The law gives the Federal Office for Immigration and Asylum (BFA)
responsibility for handling asylum applications. The BFA operated nine regional
directorates (one in each federal state) and three reception centers. In addition to
processing asylum applications, the BFA is responsible for alien police matters
(return decisions and custody pending deportation) and certain decisions on
humanitarian stays. The Federal Administrative Court in Vienna is the appeals
body for decisions of the BFA and had branches in Linz, Graz, and Innsbruck.
Access to the administrative high court is limited to cases involving principal legal
policy questions.

Following the filing of a record of more than 88,000 asylum applications in 2015,
administrative proceedings on the requests of asylum seekers from Syria, Iraq,
Afghanistan, and other countries were often lengthy. The number of applications

dropped significantly during the year, with approximately 28,800 applications filed between January and July.

In April the parliament passed a law that limits the number of asylum requests accepted for routine processing at 37,500 applications a year; the law entered into force in May. Once the cap is reached, authorities may grant asylum at the border only on the basis of specific criteria. Under this procedure authorities may accept asylum applications only from persons who argue successfully that their lives would be in danger or that they would face a real risk of torture or inhuman or degrading treatment in a neighboring country or who have a nuclear family member already in Austria. Appeals against returns would be possible only after deportation has taken place. The UN high commissioner for human rights expressed concern that asylum applicants could be rejected under the expedited procedure without having had sufficient assessment of possible grounds for asylum. NGOs and some legal experts within the country also questioned whether such measures complied with international human rights standards.

Safe Country of Origin/Transit: EU regulations provide that asylum seekers who transited a country determined to be "safe" on their way to Austria be returned to that country to apply for refugee status. Authorities considered signatories to the 1951 refugee convention and its 1967 protocol to be safe countries of transit. In response to a ruling by the European Court of Human Rights and recommendations of the UN special rapporteur on torture, the government in 2011 effectively halted the return of asylum seekers to Greece. This practice remained in effect during the year. The Federal Administrative Court ruled that deportations to Hungary would also have to be examined on an individual basis, due to the possibility of human rights violations in Hungary.

Employment: While asylum seekers are legally restricted from seeking regular employment, they are eligible for seasonal employment, low-paying community service jobs, or professional training in sectors that require additional apprentices. A work permit is required for seasonal employment but not for professional training. An employer must request the work permit for the employee.

Durable Solutions: There are provisions for integration, resettlement, and returns, which the country was cooperating with UNHCR and other organizations to improve. The integration section in the Ministry for Foreign Affairs and Integration, together with the Integration Fund and provincial and local integration offices, coordinate measures for integration of refugees. The country has a resettlement program in place for Syrian refugees. The country has bilateral agreements with several countries on implementing the return of rejected asylum seekers.

<u>Temporary Protection</u>: According to the Interior Ministry, in 2015 the government provided temporary protection to 6,803 individuals who might not qualify as refugees.

Stateless Persons

According to UNHCR there were 570 persons in the country under its statelessness mandate at the end of 2014. Stateless persons in the country were largely Austrian-born children of foreign nationals who are unable to acquire citizenship through their parents due to the laws in their parents' country of origin. Authorities did not deport them because they lacked a home country. The law allows some stateless persons to gain nationality. A stateless person born in the country may be granted citizenship within two years of reaching age 18 if he or she has lived in the country for a total of 10 years, including five years continuously before application, and are able to demonstrate sufficient income. Stateless persons could receive temporary residence and work permits that must be renewed annually.

Section 3. Freedom to Participate in the Political Process

The law provides citizens the ability to choose their government in free and fair periodic elections held by secret ballot and based on universal and equal suffrage.

Elections and Political Participation

<u>Recent Elections</u>: The country held national parliamentary elections in 2013 and presidential elections in 2016. There were no reports of serious abuse or irregularities in the 2013 election, and credible observers considered both the 2013 and the 2016 election free and fair.

In July the Constitutional Court found procedural irregularities in the May runoff vote of the presidential election that resulted in the improper counting of more than 77,900 absentee ballots. The court found no evidence of manipulation of ballots. Authorities set a repeat of the runoff election for October 2, but technical problems later discovered in voting envelopes caused authorities to delay the vote to December 4. The December repeat second round of the presidential election was generally considered to be properly administered, free, and fair. On the invitation of the government, the Organization for Security and Cooperation in Europe's Office of Democratic Institutions and Human Rights deployed an election expert team for the December 4 election, but their report was not available at the end of the year.

<u>Participation of Women and Minorities</u>: No laws limit the participation of women and members of minorities in the political process, and women and minorities did so.

Section 4. Corruption and Lack of Transparency in Government

The law provides criminal penalties for corruption by officials, and anticorruption laws and regulations extend to civil servants, public officials, governors, members of parliament, and employees or representatives of state-owned companies. The government generally implemented the law effectively. The law criminalizes corrupt practices by citizens outside the country. The penalty for bribery is up to 10 years in prison.

<u>Corruption</u>: On July 21, the Office of the Public Prosecutor for Economic Matters and Corruption filed an indictment on embezzlement and corruption charges against former finance minister Karl-Heinz Grasser and 15 other persons in connection with the 2.45 billion euro ($2.7 million) auction sale of 62,000 state-owned apartments in 2004. Prosecutors alleged that information from the Finance Ministry under Grasser's leadership helped the eventual auction winner by signaling the size of the bid that would be needed to acquire the properties. The indictment had not yet entered into force since Grasser filed several complaints against it. As a result, at year's end the trial had not started.

<u>Financial Disclosure</u>: Public officials are subject to financial disclosure laws, and there were no reports officials failed to comply with disclosure requirements. Politicians must and do publicly disclose biannually when they earn more than 1,142 euros ($1,260) for certain activities, but they are not required to disclose the amounts earned. The law does not require public officials to file disclosure reports upon leaving office. There are no sanctions for noncompliance with financial disclosure laws.

<u>Public Access to Information</u>: The law provides for full public access to government information, and the government generally respected this provision. Authorities may deny access only to information that would violate personal data protection rights by disclosing sensitive personal data on racial or ethnic origin,

political opinions, religious or philosophical beliefs, trade union membership, health, or personal life or would involve national security information. Petitioners could challenge denials of access to information before the administrative court.

Section 5. Governmental Attitude Regarding International and Nongovernmental Investigation of Alleged Violations of Human Rights

A number of domestic and international human rights groups generally operated without government restriction, investigating and publishing their findings on human rights cases. Government officials generally were cooperative and responsive to their views.

<u>Government Human Rights Bodies</u>: A human rights ombudsman's office consisting of three independent commissioners examines complaints against the government. The ombudsman's office is completely independent, has its own budget, and parliament appoints its members. The ombudsman's office effectively monitors the administration. There is a parliamentary human rights committee.

Section 6. Discrimination, Societal Abuses, and Trafficking in Persons

Women

<u>Rape and Domestic Violence</u>: Rape, including spousal rape, is punishable by up to 15 years' imprisonment. The government generally enforced the law. Law enforcement response to rape and domestic violence was effective. Women's NGOs estimated charges were filed in 10 percent of rape cases and only 13 percent of those led to convictions, due to lack of credible evidence.

Domestic violence is punishable under the criminal code provisions for murder, rape, sexual abuse, and bodily injury. There were reports of violence against women, including spousal abuse. Police can issue a two-week order barring abusive family members from contact with survivors. The order can be extended to four weeks, and a court may further extend the order.

Under the law the government provided psychosocial care in addition to legal aid and support throughout the judicial process to survivors of gender-based violence. Police training programs addressed sexual or gender-based violence and domestic abuse.

The government funded privately operated intervention centers and hotlines for victims of domestic abuse. The centers provided for victims' safety, assessed the threat posed by perpetrators, helped victims develop plans to stop the abuse, and provided legal counseling and other social services. NGOs reported these centers were generally effective in providing shelter for victims of abuse.

Sexual Harassment: The law prohibits sexual harassment, and the government generally enforced the law. Labor courts may order employers to compensate victims of sexual harassment based on the Federal Equality Commission's finding in a case. The law entitles a victim to a minimum of 1,000 euros ($1,100) in compensation.

Reproductive Rights: Couples and individuals have the right to decide the number, spacing, and timing of their children; manage their reproductive health; and have access to the information and means to do so, free from discrimination, coercion, and violence.

Discrimination: Women enjoy the same legal rights as men. Discrimination in employment and occupation occurred with respect to women.

Children

Birth Registration: By law children derive citizenship from one or both parents. Officials register births immediately.

Child Abuse: Child abuse is punishable by up to five years' imprisonment, which may be extended to 10 years if the victim dies because of negligence. Severe sexual abuse or rape of a minor is punishable by up to 20 years' imprisonment, which may be increased to life imprisonment if the victim dies because of the abuse.

The government continued its efforts to monitor child abuse and prosecute offenders. The Ministry for Economics, Family, and Youth estimated close family members or family friends committed 90 percent of child abuse. Officials noted a growing readiness to report cases of such abuse.

Early and Forced Marriage: The minimum legal age for marriage is 18. Adolescents between the ages of 16 and 18 may legally contract a marriage if they obtain a special permit for this purpose. NGOs estimated there were approximately 200 cases of early marriage annually, primarily in the Muslim and Romani communities.

<u>Sexual Exploitation of Children</u>: The law provides up to 10 years' imprisonment for an adult convicted of sexual intercourse with a child under the age of 14, the minimum age for consensual sex. If the victim becomes pregnant, the sentence may be extended to 15 years.

It is a crime to possess, trade, or privately view child pornography. Exchanging pornographic videos of children is illegal. Possession of child pornography is punishable by up to two years' imprisonment, while trading in child pornography is punishable by up to 10 years' imprisonment.

<u>International Child Abductions</u>: The country is a party to the 1980 Hague Convention on the Civil Aspects of International Child Abduction. See the Department of State's *Annual Report on International Parental Child Abduction* at travel.state.gov/content/childabduction/en/legal/compliance.html.

Anti-Semitism

According to figures compiled by the Austrian Jewish Community (AJC), there are between 12,000 and 15,000 Jews in Austria, of whom an estimated 8,000 persons are members of the AJC.

The NGO Forum against Anti-Semitism reported 465 anti-Semitic incidents during 2015. These included two physical assaults in addition to name calling, graffiti and defacement, threatening letters, dissemination of anti-Semitic writings, property damage, and vilifying letters and telephone calls. Of these, 205 cases of anti-Semitic internet postings were reported, more than double the previous year's number. The government provided protection to the AJC's offices and other Jewish community institutions in the country, such as schools and museums. The AJC noted rising fears that increasing anti-Islamic activities by the extreme right would increase anti-Semitism, with the extreme right targeting both groups as religious minorities. They also reported increasing fears of anti-Semitic activity from Muslim refugees.

In March the Vienna prosecutor's office investigated an individual who had posted anti-Semitic messages at the Vienna Jewish Museum and other Jewish institutions. There were several cases of neo-Nazi-related vandalism and hate speech, including death threats and hate speech on the internet.

School curricula included discussion of the Holocaust, the tenets of different religious groups, and advocacy of religious tolerance. The Education Ministry offered special teacher training seminars on Holocaust education and conducted training projects with the Anti-Defamation League.

Trafficking in Persons

See the Department of State's *Trafficking in Persons Report* at www.state.gov/j/tip/rls/tiprpt/.

Persons with Disabilities

The law prohibits discrimination against persons with physical, sensory, intellectual, and mental disabilities in housing, employment, education, air travel and other transportation, access to health care, the judicial system, and other government services. The government did not effectively enforce these provisions. Employment discrimination against persons with disabilities occurred.

While federal law mandates access to public buildings for persons with physical disabilities, NGOs complained many public buildings lacked such access due to insufficient enforcement of the law and low penalties for noncompliance. The Ministry of Labor, Social Affairs, and Consumer Protection handled disability-related problems. The government funded a wide range of programs for persons with disabilities, including transportation and other assistance to help integrate schoolchildren with disabilities into regular classes and employees with disabilities into the workplace.

National/Racial/Ethnic Minorities

Interior Ministry statistics released in March cited 523 neo-Nazi, right-wing extremist, xenophobic, or anti-Semitic incidents in 2015. The government continued to express concern over the activities of extreme right-wing and neo-Nazi groups, many with links to organizations in other countries.

An NGO operating a hotline for victims of racist incidents reported receiving 927 complaints in 2015. It reported that racist internet postings had nearly doubled from 2014 and had, in particular, been directed against migrants and asylum seekers, refugee shelters, and NGOs assisting them.

The Islamic Faith Community's documentation center for reporting Islamophobic incidents noted that such incidents increased markedly from only a few cases in April and May to 20 in June and July, following terrorist incidents in Western Europe.

Federal law recognizes Croats, Czechs, Hungarians, Roma, Slovaks, and Slovenes as national minorities. Human rights groups continued to report that Roma faced discrimination in employment and housing. The Austrian Romani Cultural Association estimated the Romani community consisted of more than 6,200 indigenous and between 15,000 and 20,000 nonindigenous individuals. The head of the association reported the situation of Roma continued to improve. Government programs, including financing for tutors, helped school-age Romani children move out of "special needs" programs and into mainstream classes.

NGOs reported that Africans living in the country were verbally harassed or subjected to violence in public. In some cases citizens stigmatized black Africans for perceived involvement in the drug trade or other illegal activities.

The government continued training programs to combat racism and educate police in cultural sensitivity. The Interior Ministry renewed an annual agreement with a Jewish group to teach police officers cultural sensitivity, religious tolerance, and the acceptance of minorities.

Poor German-language skills were a major factor preventing members of minorities, particularly refugees, from entering the workforce. The Labor and Integration Ministries continued efforts to improve the situation by providing German-language instruction and skilled-labor training to young persons with immigrant backgrounds. Compulsory preschool programs, including some one- and two-year pilot programs, sought to remedy language deficiencies for nonnative German speakers.

Acts of Violence, Discrimination, and Other Abuses Based on Sexual Orientation and Gender Identity

Antidiscrimination laws apply to lesbian, gay, bisexual, transgender, and intersex (LGBTI) persons. There was some societal prejudice against LGBTI persons but no reports of violence or discrimination based on sexual orientation or gender identity. Hate crime laws prohibit incitement, including incitement based on sexual orientation. LGBTI organizations generally operated freely. Civil society groups, however, criticized the lack of a mechanism to prevent service providers from discriminating against LGBTI individuals.

A 2015 Constitutional Court ruling provided for the possibility for adoption by same-sex couples as of January.

Section 7. Worker Rights

a. Freedom of Association and the Right to Collective Bargaining

The law provides the right of workers to form and join independent unions, conduct legal strikes, and bargain collectively. It prohibits antiunion discrimination or retaliation against strikers and provides for the reinstatement of workers fired for union activity. It allows unions to conduct their activities without interference. The Austrian Trade Union Federation was the exclusive entity representing workers in collective bargaining. Unions were technically independent of government and political parties, although some sectors had unions closely associated with parties.

The government effectively enforced applicable laws that covered all categories of workers. Resources, inspections, and remediation were adequate. Penalties for violations were of civil nature, with fines imposed. Administrative, registration, and judicial procedures were not overly lengthy.

There were few reports of antiunion discrimination or other forms of employer interference in union functions. The government and employers recognized the right to strike and respected freedom of association and the right to collective bargaining. Authorities enforced laws providing for collective bargaining and protecting unions from interference and workers from retaliation for union activities.

b. Prohibition of Forced or Compulsory Labor

The law prohibits all forms of forced or compulsory labor. Forced labor occurred in several sectors, such as prostitution, but also in agriculture, construction, and the catering business. Most victims were women forced into prostitution.

The government effectively enforced the law, and resources, inspections, and remediation were adequate. Labor inspectors and revenue authorities conducted routine site visits to identify forced labor. The government initiated forced labor awareness campaigns and workshops. Depending on the specific offense, penalties ranged from three to 20 years' imprisonment and were sufficient to deter most violations.

There were some trafficked migrants, both men and women, working in the agriculture, construction, and catering sectors. There were also some traffickers who subjected Romani children and persons with physical and mental disabilities to forced begging.

Also see the Department of State's *Trafficking in Persons Report* at www.state.gov/j/tip/rls/tiprpt/.

c. Prohibition of Child Labor and Minimum Age for Employment

The minimum legal working age is 15, with the exception that children who are at least 13 may engage in certain forms of light work on family farms or businesses. Children who are 15 and older are subject to the same regulations on hours, rest periods, overtime wages, and occupational health and safety restrictions as adults but are subject to additional restrictions on hazardous forms of work or for ethical reasons. Restrictions for hazardous jobs include work with materials considered dangerous for teenagers, work in the sawmill business, on high-voltage pylons, and specified jobs in the construction business.

Laws and policies protect children from exploitation in the workplace and prohibit forced or compulsory labor, and the government generally enforced these laws and policies effectively.

The labor inspectorate of the Ministry of Labor, Social Affairs, and Consumer Protection is responsible for enforcing child labor laws and policies in the workplace, and did so effectively. Penalties in the form of fines ranged from 70 to 1,090 euros ($77 to $1,200); these fines may be doubled in cases of repeated violations of the child labor code. Penalties were sufficient to deter violations.

d. Discrimination with Respect to Employment and Occupation

Labor laws and regulations related to employment or occupation prohibit discrimination regarding race, sex, gender, disability, language, sexual orientation or gender identity, HIV-positive (or other communicable disease) status, religion, age or world view (Weltanschauung). The government effectively enforced these laws and regulations.

Discrimination in employment and occupation occurred with respect to women, persons with disabilities, and members of certain minorities. A Muslim community office focused on reporting anti-Islamic acts reported discriminatory hiring practices against Muslim women wearing headscarves when trying to obtain a retail or customer service position. Companies sometimes preferred to pay a fine rather than hire a person with a disability.

The law requires equal pay for equal work. To establish greater transparency and reduce the pay gap between men and women, the government required reporting on salaries by position and gender for companies with more than 250 employees. The participation rate for women between the ages of 15 and 64 in the labor force was 67 percent, compared with 75 percent for men. Approximately 47 percent of employed women worked part time, compared with 32 percent in 2000.

Female employees in the private sector may invoke laws prohibiting discrimination against women. Depending on the Federal Equality Commission's findings, labor courts may award the equivalent of up to four months' salary to women found to have experienced gender discrimination in promotion, despite being better qualified than their competitors. The courts may also order compensation for women denied a post despite having equal qualifications.

e. Acceptable Conditions of Work

There is no legislated national minimum wage. Instead, nationwide collective bargaining agreements covered between 98 and 99 percent of the workforce and set minimum wages by job classification for each industry. The lowest bargaining agreement provided for 1,100 euros ($1,210) per month for full-time jobs. Where no such collective agreements existed, such as for domestic workers, custodial staff, and au pairs, wages were generally lower than those covered by collective bargaining agreements. The official poverty risk level was 1,163 euros ($1,280) per month.

The law provides for a maximum workweek of 40 hours, although collective bargaining agreements established 38- or 38.5-hour workweeks for more than half of all employees. Regulations to increase workhour flexibility allowed companies to increase the maximum regular time from 40 hours to 50 hours per week with overtime. In special cases work hours may be increased to a maximum of 60 hours per week, including overtime, for a maximum of 24 weeks annually. These 24 weeks, however, can only be in eight-week segments, with at least a two-week break between each eight-week period.

Overtime is officially limited to five hours per week and 60 hours per year. Authorities did not enforce these laws and regulations effectively, and some employers, particularly in the construction, manufacturing, and information technology sectors, exceeded legal limits on compulsory overtime. Sectors with immigrant workers were particularly affected. Collective bargaining agreements can specify higher limits. The law stipulates premium pay of 50 percent for overtime and requires time off for work on weekends and official holidays. An employee must have at least 11 hours off between workdays. Wage and hour violations can be brought before the labor courts that can impose fines on employers who committed the violation.

Foreign workers in both the formal and informal sectors made up approximately 13 percent of the country's workforce. Authorities did not enforce wage and hour regulations effectively in the informal sector.

The labor inspectorate regularly enforced mandatory occupational health and safety standards, which were appropriate for the main industries. Its approximately 300 inspectors routinely checked the country's nearly 210,000 worksites. Resources and remediation remained adequate. Penalties for violations range from 166 to 16,648 euros ($183 to $18,300). In the case of violations resulting in serious injury or death, the employer faces prosecution under the penal code. The government extended its Occupational Safety and Health Strategy 2007-12 initiative until 2020. The initiative focused on educational and preventive measures, including strengthening public awareness of danger and risk assessment (plus evaluation); preventing work-related illnesses and occupational diseases; training as well as information on occupational safety and health; and improving the training of prevention experts.

Workers could file complaints anonymously with the labor inspectorate, which could in turn sue the employer on behalf of the employee. Workers rarely exercised this option and normally relied instead on the nongovernmental workers' advocacy group and the Chamber of Labor, which filed suits on their behalf. Workers in the informal economy generally did not benefit from social protections. To receive health-care benefits, unemployment insurance, and pensions, workers generally had to pay into the system, although nonworkers could qualify for coverage in certain cases.

Workers can remove themselves from situations that endanger health or safety without jeopardy to their employment. The Employment and Labor Relations Federal Public Service protected employees in this situation.